Ten Town

WRITTEN BY NANCY LOEWEN • ILLUSTRATED BY RONNIE ROONEY

The Child's World

Published by The Child's World®
1980 Lookout Drive • Mankato, MN 56003-1705
800-599-READ • www.childsworld.com

ACKNOWLEDGMENTS
The Child's World®: Mary Berendes, Publishing Director
The Design Lab: Design and production
Red Line Editorial: Editorial direction

LIBRARY OF CONGRESS CATALOGING-IN-PUBLICATION DATA
Loewen, Nancy, 1964–
  Ten town / written by Nancy Loewen ;
illustrated by Ronnie Rooney.
    p. cm.
  ISBN 978-1-60253-504-6 (lib. bd. : alk. paper)
  1. Ten (The number)—Juvenile literature. 2. Number concept—
Juvenile literature. I. Rooney, Ronnie, ill. II. Title. III. Title: 10 town.
  QA141.3.L647 2010
  513.2—dc22   2010007544

Printed in the United States of America in Mankato, Minnesota.
July 2010
F11538

About the Author

Nancy Loewen has published
almost 100 books for children.
She lives in Prior Lake, Minnesota,
with 1 husband, 2 kids, 2 cats, 1 dog,
and 1 guinea pig. Altogether that's
16 eyes, 8 noses, 8 mouths, 16 ears, and
150 fingers, toes, and claws.

About the Illustrator

Ronnie Rooney was born and raised
in Massachusetts. She attended the
University of Massachusetts at
Amherst for her undergraduate study
and Savannah College of Art and Design
for her MFA in illustration. Ronnie has
illustrated numerous books for children.
She hopes to pass this love of art on to her daughter.

10

ten

In **Ten** Town, the number **10** is totally terrific!

The **10**s love **ten** so much, they cover their walls with Top **10** lists.

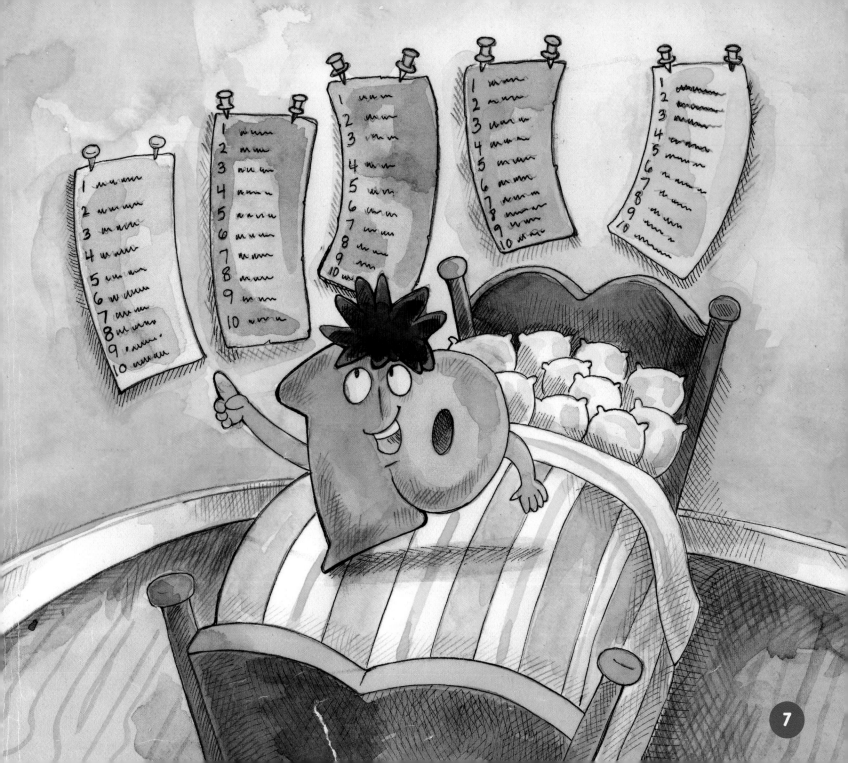

10s have two digits
(a **1** and a **0**).

That makes them feel pretty special.

Of course, getting through doors can be tricky. And chairs have to be extra wide.

The **10**s hate being mistaken for 1s.

Or worse, 0s!

School days in **Ten** Town are **ten** hours long. But those young **10**s love to learn.

After school, Tina **10** goes bowling with her friends. Each game costs **ten** cents, just like everything else in **Ten** Town.

The **10**s love to knock down all **ten** bowling pins. They love bowling because every player gets **ten** turns!

All the **10**s in **Ten** Town
are winners!

What Makes Ten?

Here are ten bowling pins. Cover one with your hand. How many are left?

Cover five bowling pins with your hand. How many are left? What number goes with 5 to make 10?

How many ways can you make ten?

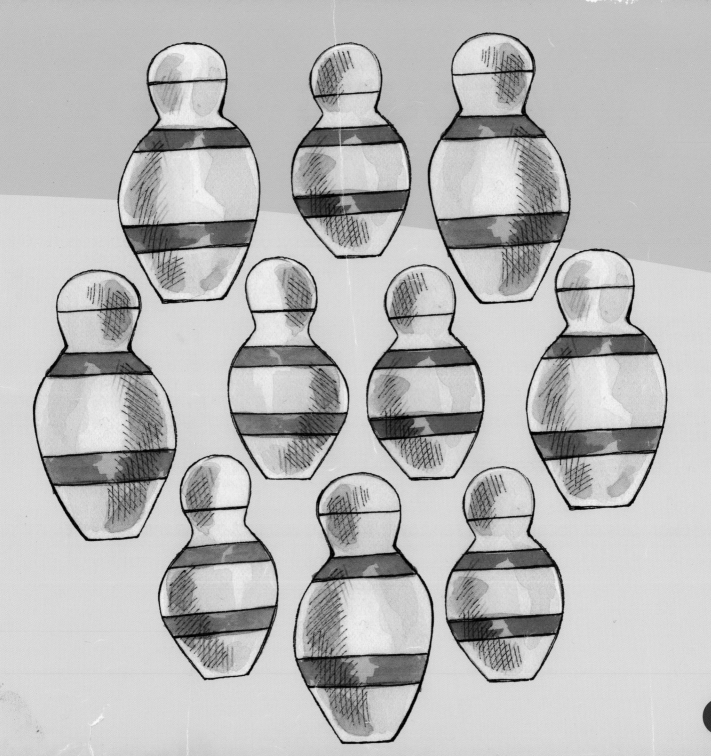

23

Know Your Numbers

Hola, 10!

In Spanish, the number "ten" is diez. Say it: *dee-AYSS*.

Time Flies

"Deca" means ten. A decade is ten years.

A Lot of Legs!

How many legs do decapods have? Ten! Crabs, lobsters, shrimp, and crayfish are examples of decapods. In Ten Town, hermit crabs are very popular pets.

One . . . Two . . . Three . . .

Have you ever heard people count to ten when they're really mad? It's a good way to take a little break and calm down.

Got It!

"10-4" is another way to say "okay" or "I understand."

Find Ten

Can you find all the things that come in tens in this book? How many groups of ten are there?